ISBN 978-1-331-88782-9
PIBN 10250049

English
Français
Deutsche
Italiano
Español
Português

www.forgottenbooks.com

Mythology Photography **Fiction**
Fishing Christianity **Art** Cooking
Essays Buddhism Freemasonry
Medicine **Biology** Music **Ancient
Egypt** Evolution Carpentry Physics
Dance Geology **Mathematics** Fitness
Shakespeare **Folklore** Yoga Marketing
Confidence Immortality Biographies
Poetry **Psychology** Witchcraft
Electronics Chemistry History **Law**
Accounting **Philosophy** Anthropology
Alchemy Drama Quantum Mechanics
Atheism Sexual Health **Ancient History**
Entrepreneurship Languages Sport
Paleontology Needlework Islam
Metaphysics Investment Archaeology
Parenting Statistics Criminology
Motivational

SIMPLIFIED SPELLING

Have you not heard how it has gone with many a cause before now? First, few men heed it; next, most men contemn it; then all men accept it—and the cause is won.

WILLIAM MORRIS.

THE SIMPLIFIED SPELLING SOCIETY
44 GREAT RUSSELL STREET
LONDON, W.C.

SIMPLIFIED SPELLING

It is the generations of children to come who appeal to us to save them from the affliction which we have endured and forgotten.—WHITNEY

WE do not know who was the first man to write a word. For long centuries language existed only as speech. The invention of written signs to represent the spoken language was a momentous advance in civilisation. It made it possible to communicate thoughts to those at a distance, far beyond the range of the voice, thoughts that would survive even when the voice of the man that conceived them had long been hushed by death.

This is not the place to discuss the gradual development of writing; how some nations came to use a sign to designate a whole word, and others used it for a syllable. The nations that we know best preferred an alphabet in which each sign represented one sound. It is clear that there are fewer different sounds than different syllables in a language, and therefore that we need fewer signs if we let each represent a sound only.

With such an alphabet, in which each sign represents one sound, and each sound has its own sign, spelling becomes a very simple matter; for if you know the sounds of a word, you can at once write the corresponding signs. For instance, if you know that the sign for the sound *b* is the letter *b*, the sign for the sound *e* is the letter *e*, and the sign for the sound *d* is the letter *d*, then on hearing the sounds of the word *bed* you know that the spelling is *bed*.

If such an alphabet is in use, then all we have to teach the child is the signs corre-sponding to the sounds.

DEFECTS OF THE PRESENT SPELLING

Let us consider whether our present English spelling can be learnt in this simple and rational fashion. Up to the point of *b e d = bed* (not a very advanced point) all is plain sailing. But take another word : The child hears the sound of *d*, the sound of *e*, and again the sound of *d*. The spelling therefore should be *ded*; but we have to inform the child that this is not the case, and that the word contains a silent *a*. On the other hand, when the child sees the word *bead*, we have to tell him that here the *a* is not silent; the two signs *ea* here have the same value as *ee* in *feed*. The child is told that the word *toe* is spelt with *oe*. But when he meets the word *toad* he is told not to spell *toed*; and when he comes to *poet* we warn him against the pronunciation *pote*. The child learns that *road* has *oa*, like *toad*; but when he proceeds to write " The man road in a carriage, and the boy road a boat," we have to explain that although the sounds are the same in these three words he must learn a different spelling for each—*road, rode, rowed.*

The child learns that the vowel in *bit* is written with the letter *i*; but he is not allowed to give the same pronunciation to the letter *i* when he meets it in *find*. In this word, he is told, the letter *i* has the same value as in *I*.

As he uses this letter in *find* and *I*, he will naturally want to use it in *my, high, eye*. But if he does so, he is assured that this is wrong. Nothing in the sound of the word *eye* shows that it should be spelt differently from *I*.

The child is told that the sounds of the word *true* are written *t r u e*. A word is uttered with another sound at the end, which he knows is written *th* ; so he spells *trueth*, only to be told that this is wrong and that here there is no *e*. Having learnt the spelling of *true*, the child hears a word in which the *t* is at the end instead of the beginning, and proceeds to write *ruet* ; wrong again. Having learnt that the spelling is *root*, he hears a word containing the same sounds, but with *f* in front ; so he writes *froot*, and has to learn that he must write *fruit*. Or, having learnt the spelling of *root*, he hears a word very much like it, but ending in *d* instead of *t*, and writes " he was *rood*." Once more the poor child has gone wrong, through no fault of his own.

Not even the consonants are represented in a consistent way. The mere sound of the word

knit does not tell us that we must write it with
k; the first sound of *sit* and of *city* is the same,
nothing shows that *s* is not right in both cases;
nothing in the sound of the words *literal* and
litter indicates that in the second case a single *t*
does not suffice to represent the sound of *t*.

It is clear that in English the sounds do not
as a rule afford trustworthy guidance to the
spelling. There are a few words like *sit*, *bed*,
lot in which the spelling is satisfactory from
this point of view; but the great majority of
common words are not spelt according to any
easily understood system, or, indeed, according
to any system whatever.

How our Spelling became what it is

This was not always the case. Long ago,
when English ceased to be only a spoken
language and came also to be written, the spelling represented the sounds in a fairly consistent
way. The *k* that people wrote in *knave*, the
gh in *night*, the *w* in *write*, were all pronounced;
so was the *e* at the end of *name*. In those days

children had little trouble in learning to spell. After a time, however, the spelling no longer represented the pronunciation in such a simple and straightforward way; and for this there were several reasons.

The pronunciation kept on changing. It is always changing, though not always at the same rate. When all the children of a country go to school and are taught reading and writing in the same way, their speech is less liable to change, especially if the spelling shows them in an unmistakable way what the sounds are. In bygone days when the schools were few and the mother tongue was neglected there was nothing to prevent the pronunciation from changing a great deal, far more than the speech of the educated does at present. But the spelling did not keep pace with the pronunciation; people went on writing certain letters even though the sounds that they once represented had changed or had disappeared.

For a time English was written by many who came from Normandy and by their descendants. They were accustomed to writing French, and when they wrote English they often represented sounds in the same way as in French. The word *house* used to be pronounced as we should pronounce it if it were written *hoos*; in French this vowel sound is written *ou* (as in the French word *tout*); and the spelling *ou* thus came to be introduced in the word *house*, taking the place of the older *u*.

When books were first printed in England the compositors often spelt the same word in different ways; there were no fixed rules. Some had learnt their trade in Holland; and memories of Dutch spelling survive in such words as *ghost*, which should have no *h* in English; *h* occurred in the Dutch word that had the same meaning.

Before long the spelling became more or less fixed. Only a few slight changes have been made in the last centuries; we no longer write *musick*, and have given up *honor* in favour of *honour* (on the advice of Dr Johnson). These changes in the spelling, however, are insignificant if we compare them with the changes that have taken place in the spoken language. The breach between the sounds and their signs has become wider and wider, until—as we have seen—the sounds have ceased to be a guide to us in spelling.

The Idea that Spelling should show the Derivation

There is, however, another way in which our spelling was rendered different from the spoken language.

In the Middle Ages Latin was held in high honour, and the mother tongue was treated with contempt. When the scholars of those days did condescend to pay some attention to English, they had the feeling that it was a very inferior language to Latin, which was used for all higher purposes, for religious worship and study, for education, and so on. They could not help noticing that some English words were connected with Latin words ; but they had undergone a change. Any change from the original Latin form was, in their eyes, manifestly a change for the worse. So they set about restoring what they could. The Latin words from which the French words are derived that gave us *debt* and *doubt* contain a *b*, so the *b* was written,—although no one pronounced it. The word *perfect* had lost its *c* (Chaucer spells it "parfit"); they put the *c* back, and after a time people actually pronounced it.

In making these changes it is clear that the true purpose of spelling—to represent the sounds and nothing else—was ignored. The written form of the word was now made a means of indicating the derivation, and it was brought closer to the spelling of the word from which it had developed.

Now the scholars of the Middle Ages knew very little of historical grammar, and consequently their activity with regard to the spelling was often quite misdirected. They wrongly thought that the word *rime* was derived from the word which has given us *rhythm*, and changed it to *rhyme*. It was imagined that *soveran* was connected with *reign*, and so it was changed to *sovereign*.

Nowadays the study of historical grammar

occupies the serious attention of many learned scholars; and they know much that was unknown or unregarded in the Middle Ages. They know that if we wanted to make words show their derivation by restoring all letters that have disappeared we should have a very difficult task; the words would become much longer than they are. It would, indeed, be impossible to tell where we should stop. Some words, for instance, have come into English from French; the French word may go back to a Latin word, which in turn may come from a Greek word.[1]   How are we to indicate all this in the spelling?   Are we to make it resemble the French word, or the Latin word, or the Greek word?   Or shall we go beyond Greek?   The Greek word itself does not give us the oldest form; scholars suggest a still older form from which they conjecture the Greek word was derived.

A language may be regarded from two points of view: as a means of communicating thought

---

[1] Thus our word *blame,* from French *blâme,* ultimately goes back to the Greek word that has also given us *blasphemy.*

and as a subject of study ; just as you can use a
horse for riding and drawing vehicles, or study
it as a zoologist does. The medieval scholars
who burdened us with such spellings as *debt*
and *sovereign* were scholars and not practical
men. They thought they were improving the
language, by making it more valuable from the
philological point of view ; they did not realise
that they were complicating the spelling and thus
rendering the written language a less simple and
satisfactory means of communicating thought.

Furthermore, most of the misspellings afford
no indication of the past history of the language,
except to the learned specialist; and even if
they did give such information to an appreciable
number of people, no one wants to know or
remember precisely what muscles a horse is
using every time he rides or drives it.

Habit has blinded us to the Defects of our Spelling

We have now seen why the spelling has
gradually ceased to be a simple representation of

the living, spoken language. We cannot help realising that it contains superfluous letters that nobody pronounces, and many ways of representing the same sounds. Yet we continue to use this spelling and make our children learn it, at great expense of time and effort.

The fact is that most of us have forgotten the time and effort it cost us when we were children. When we come to think about the early years of our school life, most of us have only hazy memories, and very few of us are able to criticise the methods that were employed by our teachers. We learnt to spell, somehow, and we went on spelling and reading words in the same spelling, year after year. The present form of words has become familiar to us—few things, indeed, could be more familiar than the form of the common words in our language. Some of them we read and write hundreds, perhaps thousands, of times every day.

Habit plays a great part in our lives. The buttons on the back of our overcoats, once used for buttoning back the full skirt, no longer serve any useful purpose; but we are content to keep

them. They would be equally useless at the
end of the coattail; but if we saw anyone with
buttons in this position, it would shock us ex-
tremely. We wear white ties with evening
dress; they are of no use, but if at a party we
met a friend without a tie we should almost
hesitate to point it out, and if we did, he would
be very uncomfortable. Our eye has become
accustomed to seeing each word always spelt in
its own peculiar way. It is accustomed to *bed*
and *dead*, to *root* and *fruit*, to *write* and *right*,
and a thousand other inconsistencies. It no
longer sees the grotesque appearance of these
words.

Probably you resent the use of the word
'grotesque.'   You would prefer to call it
'interesting' or 'picturesque.'

Just try to imagine that you had been differently accustomed; that you had learnt to spell
the language by some system that really
represented the sounds. Imagine that you had
grown accustomed to regularity and simplicity of
spelling. What would you have said to the man
who proposed to spell *tough* and *stuff*, *after* and

laughter, plough and *cow* as we actually spell
them? How would you have received the
suggestion that *det* and *dout* should be written
with *b* because the Latin words from which the
French words are derived which gave us the
English words contained a *b*—two thousand
years ago? Suppose you had been accustomed
to write *tho*, would you not have thought the
man mad who proposed to add *ugh* to it?
Suppose you had been accustomed to write *nee*,
nit and *naw*, how grotesque would you have
deemed the idea of prefixing a *k* to the first and
second, and a *g* to the third! Suppose you had
been accustomed to write *wai* and *caut*, would
you not have thought the spellings *weigh* and
caught as ludicrous as they are senseless? You
would have said: " This man is trying to spoil
the language, to disturb what we have grown
accustomed to. We like to spell the words as
we pronounce them, we like their written and
printed form. What would be the gain if we
adopted these changes? "

WHAT SHOULD WE GAIN FROM A SIMPLIFIED SPELLING?

But you have not been accustomed to a regular, simple spelling. You have learnt the spelling of words, not of sounds, and by dint of constant practice, you are able without effort to reproduce the conventional spelling. And the proposal is put to you to change that spelling, to acquire fresh habits. You are asked to consider the living, spoken language, and to write as you speak. Such a change in your habits means some temporary discomfort, that is clear. Naturally you ask: "What would be the gain if we adopted these changes?"

THE GAIN TO OUR CHILDREN

It must be said at once that the chief gain would not be yours: the change would above all benefit those who have to learn the spelling —far less, those who have learnt it. You are asked to consider this question in its bearings on the children in our schools,—not only now but through all the centuries to come,—and

B

in its bearings on British subjects and foreigners who have to learn our language.

Above all things consider our children, and especially the children who attend the elementary schools. Go into these schools and convince yourself of the vast amount of time and energy spent by the teachers and the learners alike in memorizing the spelling of words. It has been shown above that the sounds do not guide the child to the correct spelling; the spelling of hundreds upon hundreds of words has to be learnt. It is not too much to say, that from one and a half to two years of the child's school life are taken up by this memorizing. Now suppose that, instead of learning the spelling of individual words, the child had only to learn how to distinguish the sounds of the language and to produce them correctly; that we then gave him the sign or signs corresponding to each sound, and bade him spell as he pronounced. The scheme here presented can be learnt by a grown-up person in less than half an hour; let us say that a child would take three months. Does not that represent a notable saving? The school life of these children is deplorably short; are we justified in continuing to waste their time as we do at present?

There is yet another gain for the child. At present he is rarely taught to distinguish the sounds; but if we teach a spelling that depends upon the sounds, we cannot neglect them. What does this mean? It means that teachers and learners will become more observant of the spoken language, that they will pay more attention to clear speech and all that this implies—namely, good breathing, careful articulation and expressive intonation. When we listen to a man or woman who speaks clearly we are pleased; we cannot help feeling that it is too uncommon an accomplishment. Let the spelling be closely connected with the sounds, and the cultivation of the speaking voice is bound to follow.

THE GAIN TO ALL LEARNERS OF ENGLISH

English is in many respects an easy language. Its grammar is remarkably simple. Its only great weakness lies in its spelling. Nothing else stands in the way of its being the language of international intercourse. Simplify the spelling, and you make it easier for the French Canadian, for our Dutch fellow-subjects in South Africa, for the natives of India, to learn the language of the Empire. Simplify the spelling, and you increase the number of foreigners able to read and to appreciate our language. And what gain does that bring us? It means that the words written in our language, expressing our thoughts and aims, will be more widely read and better understood; it means ever-increasing influence for our journalists, novelists and dramatists, for our men of learning and our men of practical genius.

The Gain in learning Foreign Languages

It is, however, not only the foreigner learning English who would find his task lighter; the Englishman learning a foreign language would also be benefited. One of the great difficulties that besets our path when we learn a foreign language is the pronunciation. Now, of late years many have been working hard to see how the English child can best be taught the pronunciation of a foreign language ; and they have come to the conclusion that the child must know something about the sounds of English before he can be taught the sounds of French and German in the best way. This is not mere speculation ; practical experience in many schools has led to -results which would have been regarded as altogether unattainable fifteen years ago. The Modern Language teacher now has to spend much time in teaching his pupils about English sounds. If our children all learnt this when they were first taught to read and write, they would find it far easier than at present to learn the pronunciation of foreign languages.

Our Present Neglect of the Spoken Language

It is strange how the neglect of the spoken language has rendered many quite ignorant of the sounds that they utter so many times every day. People express surprise when they realise that the sound at the end of *dogs* is not *s*, but *z*; that the sound at the beginning of *thin* is not the same as that in *then*; that the first sound of *jet* is *d*; that the usual pronunciation of the vowel in *was*, *had* is not the same as that of *what* and *hat*. It has not struck them that they do not pronounce the *p* in *cupboard*, the *d* in *handkerchief*, the *t* in *castle*; and that the endings of *able* and *label*, *constant* and *persistent*, *stationary* and *stationery* are the same in sound.

Perhaps no other nation of those in the first rank is so ignorant of the sounds of the spoken language, and at the same time so respectful towards a spelling that is full of redundant letters and inconsistencies.

Every man who has made a special study of the English language will tell you that it is a thoroughly bad spelling. Professor Skeat, the most famous English scholar living, has always been a pioneer of spelling reform.

WOULD THE SIMPLIFIED SPELLING OBSCURE THE HISTORY OF WORDS?

It has probably occurred to you that if the spelling should be simplified, the history of words would be obscured. You have been thinking about the possible objections to the proposed changes, and this has struck you at once. Is your apprehension justified?

You say that you are interested in tracing derivations, that words in their present form tell you their story. How much they tell you depends on how much you know of other languages—French, German, Latin or Greek.

But what do the elementary school children know of these languages? Clearly, in their case, this argument against change would have no weight.

How many of those who learn English know more than one foreign language at all well?

Let us assume that you know French, German, Latin and Greek, and that you have a sufficient knowledge of these languages to be able to connect every English word with kindred words in these languages. Look at any passage in the simplified spelling at the end of this book; you will confess that the changes made have rarely rendered the connection obscure. Indeed, in some cases the connection becomes more clear when the spelling of a word has been simplified. *Sent* is closer to Latin *sentio* than *scent*; *muther* is closer to the German *Mutter* than *mother*; and, on the other hand, *riem* does not suggest a wrong connection with *rhythm*, as *rhyme* does.

Even granting that the simplified spelling does sometimes obscure the derivation, you must confess that your interest in the history of words is one thing, and your ordinary use of the spoken, written or printed word another. While you are talking, or reading a newspaper, or writing a letter, you are not at the same time thinking about the history of the words you use. You may occasionally let your thoughts dwell on this aspect of language, but then you look at words from quite a different point of view. Would you stand in the way of securing a great gain for the children of coming generations, because of such considerations as this?

Remember, too, that even when the simplified spelling is in general use, the present spelling, the 'old spelling' as it will then be called, will still be familiar to everybody; for the enormous number of books now in existence will not have been swept away. Everybody with any claim to education will be able to read the 'old spelling.' It will assuredly not command admiration or respect; but people will consent to read it, because of the books printed in it. No one will dream of writing it, because of the labour involved in learning the bad 'old spelling.' There will be students of the language then as now; let us hope there will be far more. To them the 'old spelling' will occasionally prove useful; but not as often as might now be thought. To the student of language a spelling that deviates so far from the pronunciation affords no very satisfactory aid in his researches. The spelling of an earlier age proves to him that *knight* and *knave* had a sounded *k*; our spelling with *k* gives no clue to the present pronunciation of these words.

It is no exaggeration to say that for one person who ever thinks of the derivation of words there are a thousand who suffer from our bad spelling; and that one in a thousand does not need the misspellings to remind him of the derivation. "The scholar does not need these indications to help him to the pedigree of the words with which he deals, and the ignorant is not helped by them; the one knows without, the other does not know with them; so that in either case they are profitable for nothing." [1]

WOULD CONFUSION ARISE FROM WORDS HAVING THE SAME SPELLING THAT ARE NOW SPELT DIFFERENTLY?

Perhaps the words *knight* and *knave* suggest another difficulty to you: if the *k* is no longer written, how are we to distinguish these words from *night* and *nave*? The words *write, right*

[1] Or, as Sainte Beuve neatly puts it: *Pour une lettre de plus ou de moins, les ignorants ne sauront pas mieux reconnaître l'origine du mot, et les hommes instruits la reconnaîtront toujours.*

and *rite*, the words *road*, *rowed*, and *rode* sound alike; will there not be confusion if the spelling is the same?

How would you answer the question: *bear* (the animal) and (I) *bear* have the same sound and the same spelling; have you ever confused them? Why not? Because the rest of the sentence makes the meaning clear. The same is true of *knight* and *night* and all the other words that sound alike but differ in meaning. When you talk about a *knight* you do not feel it necessary to pronounce the *k* to show that you mean *knight* and not *night*; and it is equally unnecessary to write the *k* for this purpose. The rest of the sentence leaves no doubt as to the meaning. In a very few cases ambiguities might arise; how rare they are you will realise if you try to construct such a sentence.

Sometimes the simplified spelling actually makes the meaning clearer. If I write the words: I *read* it, you do not know whether I mean *read* for the present or the past; in the simplified spelling the past would be *red*, in accordance with the pronunciation. A '*row* of houses' would no longer be spelt in the same way as 'making a *row*.' The noun *lead* would not have the same spelling as the verb *lead*.

OUR ATTITUDE TOWARDS REFORM

You have now come to understand that the simplification of the spelling is a matter worthy of your earnest attention. You know well that it is easy to make fun of attempts at spelling reform. The narrow-minded man, hidebound by prejudice, resents any suggestion that what is familiar to him might be changed with advantage; he likes to go on doing in his unthinking way what he has always done. He objects to change because change disturbs his comfort, and because he recoils from the mental effort required by a serious consideration of the changes proposed. He tries to thwart all attempts at improving the spelling, by pointing to this word or that in its changed form, and appealing to the prejudices of others; perhaps he even travesties the efforts of reformers by suggesting imaginary and obviously absurd spellings as likely to meet with their approval.

You, on the other hand, realise that if a real simplification could be effected, its adoption would have very important and far-reaching results; and you would like to know how we can arrive at such a simplified spelling and how we can secure its adoption.

The Problem of Spelling Reform

If we desire to improve the spelling, we can set about it in several ways; but the general principle must be to bring it into closer agreement with the sounds of the spoken language.

At first sight it would seem to be the easiest method to ascertain how many sounds we have, and to assign a letter to each. We very soon, however, meet with difficulties in the attempt to do this. We recognise that there are more sounds in English speech than there are letters in our alphabet; so that we should require new letters, or, at least, 'diacritics' (that is, accents, dots, etc.) over or under the existing letters. Additions to the alphabet are awkward, because they mean fresh types in our printing establishments, the re-modelling of typewriters, linotype machines, etc., and changes in the Morse alphabet (used in signalling, telegraphing, etc.).

But there is a more serious objection. If we use a strictly scientific phonetic alphabet, we must choose one form of English speech to the exclusion of all others. We must say that the spelling shall represent English as it is spoken in London, or in Glasgow, or in New York, or in Denver, or in Melbourne. If there were a generally recognised standard of speech, there would be no difficulty; but there is no such standard. It is quite possible that when the introduction of simplified spelling has drawn general attention to the importance of good speech, there will be a widespread desire for a standard. Even now there is some evidence of such a desire; but it is not yet strong enough to warrant us in saying: this is the best English speech, and it is to be taught in all schools, wherever English is learnt.

Many kinds of phonetic spelling have been devised. Some are used in dictionaries to indicate the pronunciation of words; others have been used particularly for the purpose of teaching foreigners the sounds of English. If you look at any of these you will find that they make extensive use either of diacritics or of new letters or of inverted letters; and that to write English in this way would change the appearance of the language very much.

Another and more promising way of solving the problem is to examine the current spelling; to consider in what ways each sound is spelt at present; and then to choose that spelling which appears to be the most common. This will give us a spelling based on present usage, containing only familiar letters and requiring no diacritics. Sometimes, it is true, we may find that two or three ways of spelling a sound are equally common; then we may choose that spelling which is most convenient for other reasons. Sometimes, too, we may find it necessary to combine two letters (to use a 'digraph') in a way which is new: for instance, our language has no convenient represeutation of the sound hear in *vision*, *measure*, and for this we may use *zh*, showing the connection of the sound with the *sh* of me*sh*.

The Representation of the Consonants

When we consider the consonants, we find that there are many which, from our point of view, are quite satisfactory; that is to say, each sound is usually represented in one way only. The sound *b* is regularly spelt *b*; the child finds it easy to remember that when he hears *bit*, the first letter of the word is a *b*. The same is true of *p*, *d*, *t*; the consonants of *bed*, *pet* give no trouble. The letters in the following words that are in bold type are also used in a satisfactory way: **m**et, **w**in, **v**ery, **f**an, **z**est, **s**o, **th**is,[1] **h**ot, **l**ot. All these letters we can adopt in our

---

[1] *Th* stands for two sounds; the *th* in *this* is not the same as the *th* in *thing*. But there is no need to differentiate these in the simplified spelling.

simplified spelling. This does not mean that we can always use them where they occur in the present spelling. The *s* of *goes* does not stand for the sound *s*, but for the sound *z*; *goes* does not rhyme with *dose*, but with *froze*. We shall therefore write *goez*. The consonant of *of* is not *f* but *v*; and we shall therefore write *ov*. The *w* in *swórd, whole, write* does not represent any sound at all; so it will be omitted. In *uphill* the letters *p* and *h* have their ordinary value; but in *phantom* the *ph* represents *f*. The sound is no guide to the present spelling. *F a n* spells *fan*; in a reasonable spelling *f a n t o m* spells the word now written with *ph*. (If those who think *ph* ought to remain because it shows the derivation from the Greek where consistent, they would write *phrenzy, phancy,* not *frenzy, fancy,* for these words also are of Greek origin.) In *nephew,* on the other hand, most of us pronounce the *ph* as *v*, and should there write *v*— which ought to please our friends the derivationists, for this brings it closer to the French *neveu,* from which it comes.

Some of the consonants are more troublesome.

c

Worst of all are the letters *c*, *k*, *qu*, *x*. Consider their present uses:

　　　　*c*at, *c*ity, o*c*ean, s*c*ience, ba*c*k.

　　　　coo*k*, bac*k*, *k*nave.

　　　　*qu*aint, *qu*ay.

　　　　e*x*tra, e*x*amine, an*x*ious.

How can the learner tell from the sounds that he must use *c* in *cat* and *k* in *kitten*? That in *cook* the same sound is first to be written *c* and then *k*? That in *taken* he must write *k*, but *c* in *bacon*?

How is he to tell from the sounds that there is an *s* in *sit*, but *c* in *city*? *s* in *sealing*, but *c* in *ceiling*?

Why should he write *ck* when *c* or *k* would suffice? Why *cocks*, but *ox*? Why *eggs*, but *examine*?

He hears the same sounds in *kill* and *quill*, except that in the second of these the *k* is followed by a *w*; why should he not write *kw* or *cw*? The sounds of *key* and *quay* are the same; how is he to tell that they differ in spelling?

The answer to all these questions is that the

learner has to learn by heart the spelling of individual words. It would assuredly be much simpler to say: when you hear the sound written *c* in *cat*, write *c* always; when you hear the sound written *s* in *sit*, write *s* always. To those who are accustomed to the present spelling, *citen* for *kitten* and *cooc* for *cook* no doubt look odd; but that is true of any change in the spelling.

The reasons for choosing *c* rather than *k* for the representation of this sound are that *c* is easier to write, and looks better than *k* (*komik, kake, kook, kolour, foks*, etc., are not attractive); and that *c* is much more common than *k*, especially at the beginning of words.

The letters *ng* in *sing* represent one sound, not two; in *anger* they represent two sounds. The same sound is written *n* in *anger* and *anchor*. While it would be more consistent to write *angger* and *angcor* or *angcer* (the *h* would, of course, disappear), it seems unnecessary to recommend a change from present usage in such cases. The spellings *anger* and *ancor* may give a little trouble to the foreigner, who may be tempted to pronounce *anger* as though it rhymed with *hanger* and *ancor, an-cor*; but to the child who knows both words by ear before he ever sees them, there is no difficulty.

The sound of *sh* in *shut* is written in many ways; consider these words: *sugar, machine, notion, special, ocean, tension, conscience, complexion, passion.* Here we have nine different ways of spelling the same sound. How is the learner to tell that *s* is to be written in *sugar*? That *ocean* and *notion, complexion* and *direction, tension* and *attention* are to be spelt as we actually spell them? Is it not a great simplification to say: when you hear the sound *sh*, write *sh*?

For the related sound that is written *s* in *measure* and *z* in *azure* the letters *zh* are suggested as the most suitable.

The sounds written *ch* in *chat* and *j* in *jet* are really *tsh* and *dzh*; but the present spelling *ch* and *j* is more convenient. We write *ch* in *which* and *tch* in *witch*; it is simpler to say: write *ch* always when you hear it. The sound of *j* appears in *jet*, but also in *gem, wager, badger, badge, legion, spinach.* The learner cannot tell which of these spellings is correct in any particular word; he has to learn the spelling of each word separately. It would be far simpler to give the rule: write the letter *j* when you hear the sound of *j*.

We have now dealt with the sounds:

bet	pet	dip	tip	got	cot
met	net	sing	*N.B.*—linger		thinc
win	van	fan	this	thing	
zest	so	vizhon	sheen	jest	cheer
liv	hapy				

The only consonants that remain to be considered are *y*, *r*, and *wh*.

In the present spelling *y* is used for three purposes. It represents a consonant in *yet*, and it may well be retained with this value. It also represents vowels, in *physics*, *city* and in *type*; the *y* in physic, city has the same value as *i* in v*i*sit, cit*i*zen, and the *y* in type, why has the same value as *ie* in cr*ie*s. We shall meet with these sounds again when we come to the vowels.

The letter *r* has various pronunciations in different parts of the English-speaking world, and it will be well to keep it where it occurs in the present spelling, even in words where some have ceased to pronounce it.

The letters *wh* are also variously pronounced. In some parts there is no 'difference between *wh* and *w*; *which* is pronounced like *witch*, *where* like *wear*, *while* like *wile*. As, however, so many speakers of English do make a distinction, it will be well to keep *wh* where it occurs in the present spelling.

From what has gone before, you will see that the consonants on the whole present little difficulty; and that is a very important fact. In our language they are more numerous than the vowels; and it is not difficult to read a sentence in which only the consonants have been written and the vowels have been left out.[1] The consonants are a much more stable element in language than the vowels.

---

[1] As an example, take the sentence :
e **ai* **a* a* ***ee o**o** o* *ue**ay* a** **u***ay*
and compare it with :
Th* tr**n st*rts *t thr** *cl*ck *n T**sd**s *nd Th*rsd**s.

DOUBLE CONSONANTS AND SILENT CONSONANTS

Before passing to the vowels, we must pay a little attention to the double consonants and the silent consonants.

When we say the word *coattail* we pronounce the *t* at the end of *coat* and the *t* at the beginning of *tail*. But the case is different in *written*; we only pronounce one *t* here. We pronounce both *p's* in *lamppost*, but only one in *happy*. In *bigger* we pronounce one *g* only, just as in *figure*. In *all* we pronounce one *l*, just as in *awl*. In *muddy* we pronounce one *d*, just as in *study*. It is clear that where the consonant is only pronounced once, it should be written only once.

Silent consonants occur in a fair number of words, for instance in *light, whole, gnat, knave, write, lamb, autumn, science, sign, half, doubt, answer, yacht*. Where a letter represents no sound at all, it cannot be retained in a simplified spelling.

Short Vowels

The short vowels fortunately give little trouble. You will accept without hesitation the spelling of them as it occurs in *glad, bet, lily, song, good* and *bud.* If this use of *a, e, i* (*y* finally [1]), *o, oo, u* [2] be made regular for the short vowels, some changes will of course result. The silent *u* will have to disappear from *guest,* and you will write *gest* as you write *best*; you remember that we are giving *g* uniformly the value it has in *go,* and *gest* will therefore not be confused with *jest.* You will write *frend* (cp. *lend*), *hed* (cp. *bed*), *forin* (cp. *florin*), *uther* (cp. *utter*), *flud* (cp. *bud*).

Long Vowels and Diphthongs

The long vowels and diphthongs present far more difficulty, for their spelling is very varied. To give all the different ways in which these sounds are at present spelt would take up a great deal of space ; it will be sufficient for our present purpose to give a few examples, and to

---

[1] Some may prefer to write *i* in final positions also.

[2] For *u* as in *volume,* see p. 45.

indicate which spelling of these sounds appears to be the most convenient.

Let us take as our first example the sound of *o* in *go*, which some pronounce as a long vowel, others as a diphthong, others again as a diphthong of another kind. The following words show thirteen different ways of writing this *o*:

Go, goes, road, rode, row, rowed, mauve, bureau, yeoman, sew, brooch, though, soul.

They are, of course, not all equally common; but each of the spellings exemplified by *go, goes, road, rode* and *row* occurs in many words.

As a second example we may take the long sound of *u* in *truth*. The following words show ten different spellings of this sound:

truth, true, rule, fruit, rheumatism, drew, mood, through, move, shoe.

Our third example shall be the sound of *ie* in *cries*. The following words show eleven different spellings of this sound:

cries, dial, high, height, file, cry, type, aisle, guide, buy, eye.

These examples serve to show that nowhere is simplification more urgently needed than in the case of the long vowels and diphthongs; at the same time it is obvious that the number of changes will be the greatest. In the following suggestions for a simplified spelling of these sounds, the attempt has been made to produce a system that is easy to learn and that takes into account, as far as possible, what is most common in the present spelling. The problem has been very earnestly considered by persons who are familiar with all its aspects, and after prolonged deliberations the following scheme has been evolved:

(i) Write *aa* in faather, *ar* in far.

(ii) Write *ai* in maid, *air* in fair.

(iii) Write *au* in laud, *or* in lord.

(i) If we used the single *a* we should get into difficulties; thus we are bound to drop the silent *l* in *calm, palm,* etc., but we cannot write *cam, pam.* We have the digraph *aa* in the present spelling of the word 'bazaar.' Although some make no difference in pronunciation between *father* and *farther*, many do; and the distinction must therefore be kept in the spelling and the *r* retained in the latter word.

Some do not say *faast* but *fast* (with the same vowel as in *fat*); these would naturally write this and similar words with one *a* only.

(ii) It is clear that the present *made* and *maid* will have the same spelling; *day* will be written *dai*, *great* will become *grait*; *there* and *their* will become *thair*, *bear* and *bare*: *bair*. On the other hand *pail*, *pair*, *maid*, *pain*, and many other words will remain unchanged.

(iii) *Haul*, *haunt*, *caught*, etc., will retain their *au*; but in other words a change will be necessary. Thus we shall have *baul*, *clau*, *braud*, *baut*, *thaut*. *Or* will remain in *form*, *port*, *orb*, and many other words; but *more* will become *mor*.

(iv) Write *ee* in feel, but write *e* ⎫
(v) Write *ie* in liet, but write *i* ⎪ before an-
(vi) Write *oe* in loed, but write *o* ⎬ other vowel
(vii) Write *uu* in truuth, but write *u* ⎪ or at the end
(viii) Write *yue* in yueth, but write *yu* ⎭ of a word.

(iv) We shall then be no longer troubled by such difficulties as *speak* and *speech*, which will look much more closely related as *speec* and *speech*; *feet* and *feat* will have the same spelling, as also *beet* and *beat*, *meet* and *meat*. (As was shown

on p. 27, this can hardly ever lead to ambiguity.)
The single letter *e* is found to be sufficient when
a vowel follows, as in *theory*; and when the sound
is at the end of a word, as in *he, she, we, me, be.*

(v) The sound of *ie* in *cries* has many different spellings, as was shown on p. 41. No one
spelling is at present more common than any
other, unless it be the spelling of which *wide*
is an example. This kind of spelling, by means
of a mute *e* following a consonant, is for various
reasons unacceptable. The spelling *ie* is the
one that fits best into a complete scheme of the
vowels, and as in the case of *ee*, the first letter
only need be written before vowels and at the
end of a word, e.g. *dial, I, mi, whi.*

(vi) Much the same considerations lead to
the adoption of *oe* for the sound in *goes.* Here,
too, *o* suffices before other vowels (as in *heroic*)
and finally (as in *no, so, go*).

(vii and viii) Quite the most difficult problem
in connection with the vowels was to determine
the best spelling of the sounds written *ue* in
true and *cue* respectively. The present spelling
is most confusing. For *ue* in *true* this was

shown on p. 41 ; as for *ue* in *cue*, it is now spelt
in at least ten different ways :

*cue, cubic, cube, suit, eulogy, adieu, few, view,
beauty, ewe.*

After many proposals had been considered it
was decided that *uu* was the most acceptable
spelling for the sound of *u* in *truth*, and that *u*
alone would suffice before another vowel (as
in *ruin*) and finally (as in *tru*) ; and that *yue* was
the best spelling for the sound of *u* in *duty*, *yu*
sufficing when a vowel follows (as in *dyual*) or
finally (as in *dyu*),—also in uustressed syllables
as in *volyum*) This was one of the very few
cases in which the present spelling did not afford
convenient means of designating the sounds.

(In some forms of English, the distinction
between the long sound (as in *mood*) and the
short sound (as in *good*) will at first give some
trouble, just as in other forms of English the
distinction between the sounds of *laud* and
lord, *father* and *farther*. It is probable that
distinctions made in the simplified spelling will
soon lead to a slightly modified pronunciation
in such cases.)

(ix) Write *oi* in coin.

(x) Write *ou* in count.

There could be little doubt about the spelling of these diphthongs. It is true that at the end of words the present spelling generally has *oy* and *ow*; but to make this a rule would be a useless complication.

(xi) Write *ur* in fur (*i.e.* in stressed positions).

(xii) Write *er* in sister (*i.e.* in unstressed positions).

(xi and xii) Most speakers make no difference in pronunciation between *er* in *fern* and *ur* in *burn*, *er* in *herb* and *ur* in *curb*, *ir* in *bird* and *ur* in *absurd* and *or* in *word*. The most common spelling is *ur*, which has therefore been selected; another reason was the close relation of this sound to the *u* in *but*. There can be little doubt that the *er* in *sister* should be retained with its present value.

Vowels in Unstressed Syllables

The question how far the use of *er* should be extended is most difficult to answer, for it compels us to face the problem of the vowels in unstressed syllables. Take the following examples :

able and *label*; *idle* and *idol*; *mettle* and *metal.*

tailor and *trailer*; *alter* and *altar*; *beggar* and *bigger*; *stationery* and *stationary.*

balsam and *venom*; *infamy*, *enemy* and *economy*; *infamous* and *blasphemous.*

ocean and *notion*; *musician* and *position.*

barren and *baron*; *gotten* and *cotton.*

distant and *persistent*; *distance* and *sentence*; *tenancy* and *clemency.*

Read these words in a natural way; you will find it easier to do this if you introduce them into sentences. It is probable that you will then realise that our spelling shows a variety of vowel letters where in our ordinary pronunciation only one vowel sound is heard. This 'obscure' or 'neutral' vowel, as it is called, is of frequent occurrence in English, as also in French and German. In a purely phonetic alphabet it is usually represented by the sign ə (an inverted e).

You may, however, have noticed that public

speakers who are very deliberate and precise in their speech do make distinctions in some of the cases of which examples have been given above; and there are many who believe that this is a practice to be commended and worthy of general imitation and extension. They maintain that this adds to the beauty of the language, and that the variety of the vowel letters, as found in the present spelling of unstressed endings, should be indicated in the pronunciation also; so that, for instance, the second syllable of *moment* would be pronounced like *meant* (which is, indeed, done by a good many) and that the second syllable of *idol, sailor* should be pronounced like *doll, lore* respectively. They also maintain that in many cases it is desirable to retain the present spelling of the vowel because of the existence of derived words in which the vowel is stressed and appears with its full value, *e.g. metal* and *metallic, idol* and *idolatry, baron* and *baronial, ocean* and *oceanic.*

Others, however, regard such a pronunciation of the unstressed vowels as an unwarrantable revival of what has long disappeared. They say that the reduction of the vowels in unstressed syllables, far from being a sign of deterioration, is a sign of progress; that what has taken place, for instance, in German and other kindred languages, has its justifiable parallel in our own. In other languages this development shows itself in the spelling as well as in the spoken language; for instance, the *e* in German *Bruder leider Häuser* goes back to various vowels, which ceased to be differentiated in the spelling when the ' neutral ' vowel had taken their place in the spoken language. They also point to the usage of the poets, who may surely be regarded as not indifferent to the beauty of the language, but who do not hesitate to use such rhymes as *splendid, attended* (Wordsworth), *ever, endeavour* (Wordsworth, Byron), *sever, endeavour* (Th. Moore), *tender, splendour* (Shelley), *motion, ocean* (Wordsworth, Coleridge, Shelley), *sentence, repentance* (Byron), *heaven, Devon* (Tennyson), *languors, angers* (Tennyson).

There is another vowel that appears commonly in unstressed syllables, a vowel which resembles

D

the *i* of *pit*.   The following examples show the present spellings of this sound :

city and *citizen*; *carry* and *carrier*; *captain* and *satin*; *roses* and *posies*; *volley* and *folly*; *purest* and *purist*; *postage, vestige,* and *privilege.*

The practical question for us is : How are we to deal with the vowels in unstressed syllables in our scheme of simplified spelling?   It is impossible to tell which of the two incompatible views stated above will win the day; time alone can decide.   In these circumstances it will be wise to retain for the present any differences which may survive, not only in the spelling, but in very precise speech.   Those who prefer a spelling more in accordance with their natural speech (by no means the same thing as 'careless' or 'slipshod' speech) should be at liberty to use it.

The Simplified Spelling in Brief

We have now dealt with the sounds of the English language and their representation by means of a simple and reasonably consistent spelling, of which this table gives a summary:

CONSONANT SOUNDS

bet	pet	dip	tip	got	cot
met	net	sing	N.B.—linger, thinc		
win	whim	van	fan	this	thing
zest	so	vizhon	sheen	jest	cheer
left	riet	yes	hapy		

VOWEL SOUNDS

glad best lily	song	bud	good	volyum
faather star	maid	fair	land	lord

leed, seing, wo   liet, dial, mi   loed, going, no   buun, juel, thru   yueth, dyual, dyu

joi   mount   curl   sister

Realize that when the child has learnt to distinguish the sounds, this little table gives him the way in which they are to be spelt. Then turn to any book now in use for teaching our spelling and ask yourself which is the more economical system. If it implied economy at the expense of educational soundness, you would rightly give it no further attention. That it is educationally sound has been shown above; but it will be well to give here, in a few words, the advantages of this system of simplified spelling.

ADVANTAGES OF THE SIMPLIFIED SPELLING

It is easy to learn. Try for yourself. Say a sentence and then write it in simplified spelling. If you do find difficulty, it is because you have not been accustomed to distinguish the sounds you utter, because in childhood your ear-training was neglected.

It can be taught by rational methods. The process will be this : The attention of the child is drawn to the sounds he uses in speaking. His organs of speech as well as his ears are trained. Then he learns to represent the sounds by letters. He does not learn the spelling of individual words, which calls for excessive memorising. (There are other and far better ways of practising the memory.)

The training of the ear and of the vocal organs which is an essential part of learning the simplified spelling is of great value. It is useful in leading to clearer speech, and forms the basis of all good work in elocution and singing. It is the best preparation for learning shorthand. It affords great help in mastering the pronunciation of foreign languages. There is no doubt that the simplification of spelling would very soon lead to a great improvement in pronunciation. Slovenliness and vulgarity are fostered by the lack of a clear and constant relation between the written symbol and the spoken sound.

One who has learnt the simplified spelling will be able to read books in the 'old spelling' with little trouble. Many words are the same. In devising the simplified spelling care has been taken to make the least possible change that is consistent with efficiency. After a little practice, it would be quite easy to *read* the 'old spelling'; but no one would be expected to *write* it, and it is this which requires so much effort.

It is easy to print. As it contains no new letters and no diacritics, existing founts of type will serve perfectly. There is no need to effect any change in typewriters, linotype machines, etc. The alphabet used in telegraphy and in signalling will remain the same.

It makes English the most serviceable language

for intercourse within the Empire and between nations. No other language offers the same combination of advantages as ours. It has a very simple grammar and a very rich vocabulary; it is the key to a grand literature. Its only serious drawback is—the spelling.

If we agree to make the spelling of English as reasonable and straightforward as is that of Spanish, or even of German, we shall confer an inestimable boon on the children of untold generations to come. We shall add to the efficiency of all English-speaking peoples by effecting an immense improvement in elementary education, by which every child, rich or poor, will be the gainer. We shall ensure the continued spread of the English language throughout the world.

How You can Help the Movement for Reform

When you look at the names of those who are interesting themselves in the movement, when you see that men like Sir James Donaldson,

Professor Gilbert Murray, Sir Frederick Pollock, Sir William Ramsay, Professor Michael Sadler, Professor Skeat, to mention only a few, are keen members of the Simplified Spelling Society, you may be inclined to say: I may well leave the work to these men. That, however, is not what they want at all. They may be able to do more than you, but they cannot dispense with your active support. Like every other great movement, it appeals to all educated men and women. We want your personal interest, we want your help in the campaign for simplified spelling.

You can help us a great deal. Think about the questions involved, talk about them to your friends, take an interest in the spoken language. When you meet with ignorance and prejudice, do your utmost to dispel these enemies to all open-minded consideration of the problem. The arguments that you will have to answer are always the same.

Brief Answers to the Arguments of Opponents

The simplified spelling looks queer, ugly, etc.
Answer: Prejudice, born of habit. Familiarity, in this case, breeds ill-placed admiration. Those brought up on the simplified spelling will be just as devoted to that, and with better cause.[1]

Words of the same sound now spelt differently would be spelt alike, which would lead to confusion.

[1] You may perhaps hear someone exclaim: "Shakespeare's spelling is good enough for me." We happen to have no evidence as to Shakespeare's spelling—except that he was not particular as to the spelling of his name ; here is an example of Shakespeare's printers' spelling :

> How fweet the moone-light fleepes vpon this banke,
> Heere will we fit, and let the founds of muficke
> Creepe in our eares, foft ftilnes and the night
> Become the tutches of fweet harmonie.

Or again some one may say: "I should not like to see the Bible in simplified spelling." Probably he would not, at first ; and it is also probable that he would not like it in the spelling of the sixteenth century. After all, it is the meaning that matters ; and those accustomed to reading the Bible in the simplified spelling would revere its teaching no less than we do.

Answer: There is no confusion when the words are spoken; why should there be any when they are written? The context makes the meaning clear. Some words, now spelt alike, would be differentiated.

A change of spelling would obscure the derivation.

Answer: Granted, sometimes; in other cases it would make it clearer. In our ordinary use of language we are not at the same time studying etymology; for the student of etymology the 'old spelling' will still be available for reference.

It is good for children to work hard.

Answer: Of course it is; and there are plenty of subjects of great intrinsic importance at which they can work hard. But where is the intrinsic importance of writing *tho, though* and *frend, friend*? To compel them to learn all the redundancies and inconsistencies of our spelling because of the hard work involved is as sensible as to make them write with their feet rather than with their hands because of the harder work entailed in doing so.

Brief answers have been given here ; but all these objections have been dealt with on earlier pages of this book, except the last,—which is really too contemptible to call for an extensive answer.

ADOPTION OF THE SIMPLIFIED SPELLING

You may also like to show that you are a friend of progress by making use of the simplified spelling in your letters or in print. The more often people see words spelt in the reasonable way, the more quickly will they get accustomed to the idea of change.

Possibly, however, you may prefer to wait until the scheme is more widely known before adopting it in its complete form. In the meantime you may be willing to adopt certain obvious simplifications which form part of the proposed scheme. The following rules are suggested for provisional use :

1. Drop silent letters when this does not involve a change of pronunciation ; *e.g.* write *dout* for *doubt*, *activ* for *active*, *definit* for

definite, *program* for *programme*, *pich* for *pitch*, but not *brit* for *bright*. (Do not adopt *brite*, which is contrary to the spelling *ie* suggested for this diphthong in the scheme.)

2. Where a consonant is doubled in a simple word (not in a compound), drop one letter when this does not involve a change in pronunciation, *e.g.* write *batl* for *battle*, *teror* for *terror*, *begining* for *beginning*, but keep the two letters in *coattail*, *lamppost*, *interrupt*, *batted*, *latter*. (The forms *bated*, *later* in the present spelling do not have this value, and confusion would arise.)

3. Write *t* in place of the ending *ed* of many verbs, whenever *t* represents the pronunciation; *e.g. past* for *passed*, *prest* for *pressed*.

4. Substitute *f* for *ph*.

THE SIMPLIFIED SPELLING SOCIETY

Finally, you can show your interest in the movement by joining the Simplified Spelling Society, the office of which is at 44 Great Russell Street, London, W.C. However limited your means may be, you will be able to subscribe one shilling a year, which makes you an Associate Member; this subscription assures us of your moral support, which we value highly. If you can afford five shillings a year, this payment will make you a full Member, and will help the Society to extend its work. It is no easy task that we have taken in hand; our appeal is to millions, scattered all over the earth. We want to establish branches in every important centre where English is spoken. We want to gain the sympathetic help of every newspaper. We want to dispel prejudice and prepare the path for reform. A great undertaking needs money, and we appeal without hesitation for pecuniary help to those who can afford it. But to all, rich and poor alike, we appeal for the earnest consideration of the case for simplified spelling which has been put forward in these pages; we believe that there are few causes more worthy of support than this, which aims at the prevention of waste in our schools, at better educational methods and at rendering more serviceable for all the English language.

SPECIMENS OF SIMPLIFIED SPELLING

THE following pages contain a short story by Dickens and the ballad of "John Gilpin." A perusal of them will give a good idea of the results of simplifying the spelling in the way that has been suggested. Proper names have, of course, been left unchanged.

The reader will experience little difficulty in reading the simplified spelling; such difficulties as may occur will probably be due not so much to the spelling as to his unfamiliarity with some of the features of our pronunciation.

Naturally he will at first receive shock upon shock as he meets with words in strange guise, but as he reads on, he will quickly grow accustomed to the spelling, and he will probably soon realize that this spelling suggests the spoken language to him in a manner quite unexpected and surprising.

If, after reading these pages, he attempts to make use of the simplified spelling himself, he will be astonished to see how easily he can do so. It is no exaggeration to say that an educated person can learn the simplified spelling in half an hour.

BEING raather yung at prezent—I am geting on in yeerz, but stil I am raather yung—I hav no particyular adventyurz ov mi oen tu faul bac upon. It woodn't much interest enibody heer, I supoez, tu no whot a scru the Reverend iz, or whot a grifin *she* iz, or hou thai du stic it intu pairents—particyularly hair-cuting and medical atendans. Wun ov our feloez woz charjd in hiz haaf's acount twelv and sicspens for tu pilz—tolerably profitabl at sics and threepens a pees, I shood thinc — and he never tooc them iether, but put them up the sleev ov hiz jacet.

Az tu the beef, it's shaimful. It's not beef. Regyular beef izn't vainz. Yu can chu regyular beef. Besiedz which, thair'z graivy tu regyular beef, and yu never se a drop tu ourz. Anuther ov our feloez went hoem il, and hurd the family doctor tel hiz faather that he coodn't acount

for hiz complaint unles it woz the beer. Ov
cors it woz the beer, and wel it miet be!

Houever, beef and Oeld Cheeseman ar tu
diferent thingz. So iz beer. It woz Oeld
Cheeseman I ment tu tel about; not the maner
in which our feloez get thair constityueshonz
destroid for the saic ov profit. Whi, looc at
the pi-crust aloen. Thair'z no flaicines in it.
It's solid—liec damp led. Then our feloez get
nietmairz, and ar boelsterd for cauling out and
waicing uther feloez. Hu can wunder!

Oeld Cheeseman wun niet wauct in hiz sleep,
poot hiz hat on oever hiz nietcap, got hoeld ov
a fishing-rod and a cricet-bat, and went doun intu
the parlor, whair thai natyuraly thaut from hiz
apeerans he woz a goest. Whi, he never wood
hav dun that if hiz meelz had been hoelsum.
When we aul begin tu wauc in our sleeps, I
supoez thai'l be sory for it.

Oeld Cheeseman wozn't second Latin Maaster
then; he woz a felo himself. He woz furst
braut thair, very smaul, in a poest shaiz, bi a
wooman hu woz alwaiz taicing snuf and shaicing
him—and that woz the moest he rememberd

about it. He never went hoem for hiz holidaiz.
Hiz acounts (he never lurut eny ecstraz) wer sent
tu a Banc, and the Banc paid them; and he had a
broun syuet twies a yeer, and went intu buuts at
twelv. Thai wer alwaiz tu big for him, tu.

In the Midsumer holidaiz, sum ov our feloez
hu livd within waucing distans, yuest tu cum bac
and cliem the treez outsied the plaiground waul,
on purpos tu looc at Oeld Cheeseman reeding
thair bi himself. He woz alwaiz az mield az
the te—and that's prety mield, I shood hoep!
—so when thai whisld tu him, he looct up
and noded; and when thai sed, "Halo, Oeld
Cheeseman, whot hav yu had for diner?" he
sed "Boild muton"; and when thai sed, "Ain't
it solitary, Oeld Cheeseman?" he sed, "It's a litl
dul sumtiemz"; and then thai sed, "Wel, good
bi, Oeld Cheeseman!" and cliemd doun again.
Ov cors it woz impoezing on Oeld Cheeseman
tu giv him nuthing but boild muton thru a
hoel vacaishon, but that woz just liec the sistem.
When thai didn't giv him boild muton, thai gaiv
him ries pooding, pretending it woz a treet.
And saivd the boocher.

E

So Oeld Cheeseman went on. The holidaiz braut him intu uther trubl besiedz the loenlines; becauz when the feloez began tu cum bac, not wonting tu, he woz aulwaiz glad tu se them; which woz agravaiting when thai wer not at aul glad tu se him, and so he got hiz hed noct against waulz, and that woz the wai hiz noez bled. But he woz a faivorit in jeneral. Wuns a subscripshon woz raizd for him; and, tu ceep up hiz spirits, he woz prezented befor the holidaiz with tu whiet mies, a rabit, a pijon, and a byuetiful pupy. Oeld Cheeseman cried about it —espeshaly sunn aafterwerdz, when thai aul et wun anuther.

At laast, Oeld Cheeseman woz maid second Latin Maaster. He woz braut in wun morning at the begining ov a nyu haaf, and prezented tu the scuul in that capasity az "Mr Cheeseman." Then our feloez aul agreed that Oeld Cheeseman woz a spi and a dezurter, hu had gon oever tu the enemy'z camp, and soeld himself for goeld. It woz no ecscyues for him that he had soeld himself for very litl goeld—tu pound ten a cworter and hiz woshing, az woz reported. It woz desieded bi a Parliment which sat about it, that Oeld Cheeseman'z mersenary moetivz cood aloen be taicen intu acount, and that he had " coind our blud for dracmaz." The Parliment tooc the ecspreshon out ov the cworel seen between Brutus and Cassius.

When it woz setld in this strong wai that Oeld Cheeseman woz a tremendus traitor, hu had wurmd himself intu our feloez seecrets on purpos tu get himself intu faivor bi giving up everithing he nyu, aul curaijus feloez wer invieted tu cum forwerd and enroel themselvz in a Soesiety for maicing a set against him. The Prezident ov the Soesiety woz Furst Boi, naimd Bob Tarter. Hiz faather woz in the West Indies, and he oend himself that hiz faather woz wurth Milionz. He had grait pouer amung our feloez, and he roet a parody, begining,

" Hu maid beleev tu be so meec
That we cood hardly heer him speec,
Yet turnd out an Informing Sneec ?
Oeld Cheeseman."

—and on in that wai thru mor than a duzen vursez, which he yuest tu go and sing, every morning, cloes bi the nyu maaster'z desc. Aul this prodyuest a grait efect on Oeld Cheeseman. He had never had much hair; but whot he had, began tu get thiner and thiner every dai. He gru pailer and mor worn; and sumtiemz ov an eevening he woz seen siting at hiz desc with a preshus long snuf tu hiz candl, and hiz handz befor hiz fais, criing. But no member ov the Soesiety cood pity him, even if he felt incliend, becauz the Prezident sed it woz Oeld Cheeseman'z conshens.

He had oenly wun frend in the wurld, and that wun woz aulmoest az ponerles az he woz, for it woz oenly Jane. Jane woz a sort ov wordroeb wooman tu our feloez, and tooc cair ov the bocsez. She had cum at furst, I beleev, az a ciend ov aprentis—sum ov our feloez sai from a Charity, but *I* doen't no—and aafter her tiem woz out, had stopt at so much a yeer. So litl a yeer, perhaps I aut tu sai, for it iz far mor liecly. Houever, she had poot sum poundz in the Saivingz Banc, and she woz a very nies yung wooman. She woz not cwiet prety, but she had a very franc, onest, briet fais, and aul our feloez wer fond ov her. She woz uncomonly neet and cheerful, and uncomonly cumfortabl and ciend. And if enithing woz the mater with a felo'z muther, he aulwaiz went and shoed the leter tu Jane. Jane woz Oeld Cheeseman'z frend. The mor the Soesiety went against him, the mor Jane stood bi him. She yuest tu giv him a goodhyuemord looc out ov her stilroom windo, sumtiemz, that seemd tu set him up for the dai. She yuest to paas out ov the orchard and the cichengarden (aulwaiz cept loct, I beleev yu!) thru the plaiground, whcn she miet hav gon the uther wai, oenly tu giv a turn ov her hed, az much az tu sai, "Ceep up yuer spirits!" tu Oeld Cheeseman. Hiz slip ov a room woz so fresh and orderly that it woz wel noen hu looct aafter it whiel he woz at hiz desc; and when our feloez sau a smoecing hot dumpling on hiz plait at diner, thai nyu with indignaishon hu had sent it up.

Under theez surcumstansez, the Soesiety re-zolvd, aafter a cwontity ov meeting and debait-ing, that Jane shood be recwested tu cut Oeld Cheeseman ded; and that if she refyuezd, she must be sent tu Coventry herself. So a depyutaishon, heded bi the Prezident, woz apointed tu wait on Jane, and inform her ov the voet the Soesiety had been under the painful nesesity ov paasing. She woz very much respected for aul her good cwolitiz, and thair woz a story about her having wuns wailaid the Reverend in hiz oen study, and got a felo of from seveer punishment, ov her oen clend cumfortabl hart. So the depyutaishon didn't much liec the job. Houever, thai went up, and the Prezident toeld Jane aul about it. Upon which Jane turud very red, burst intu teerz, informd the Prezident and the depyutaishon, in a wai not at aul liec her yuezhyual wai, that thai wer a parsel ov malishus yung savajez, and turnd the hoel respected body out ov the room. Consecwently it woz enterd in the Soesiety'z booc (cept in astronomical siefer for feer ov detecshon), that aul commyunicaishon with Jane woz interdicted; and the Prezident adrest the memberz on this convinsing instans ov Oeld Cheeseman'z undermiening.

But Jane woz az tru tu Oeld Cheeseman

az Oeld Cheeseman woz fauls tu our feloez—
in thair opinion, at aul events—and stedily
continyud tu be hiz oenly frend. It woz a
grait egzaasperaishon tu the Soesiety, becauz
Jane woz az much a los tu them az she woz
a gain tu him; and being mor inveterait
against him than ever, thai treeted him wurs
than ever. At laast, wun morning, hiz desc
stood emty, hiz room woz peept intu, and
found tu be vaicant, and a whisper went about
amung the pail faisez ov our feloez that Oeld
Cheeseman, unaibl tu bair it eny longer, had
got up urly and dround himself.

The misteerius loocs ov the uther maasterz
aafter brecfast, and the evident fact that Oeld
Cheeseman woz not ecspected, confurmd the
Soesiety in this opinion. Sum began tu discus
whether the Prezident woz liabl tu hanging
or oenly transportaishon for lief, and the
Prezident's fais shoed a grait angziety tu no
which. Houever, he sed that a juury ov hiz
cuntry shood fiend him gaim; and that in hiz
adres he shood poot it tu them to lai thair
handz upon thair harts and sai whether thai

az Britonz apruuvd ov informerz, and hou thai thaut thai wood liec it themselvz. Sum ov the Soesiety considerd that he had beter run awai until he found a forest whair he miet chainj cloethz with a woodcuter and stain hiz fais with blacberiz; but the majority beleevd that if he stood hiz ground, hiz faather—belonging az he did tu the West Indies, and being wurth Milionz—cood bi him of.

Aul our feloez harts beet faast when the Reverend caim in, and maid a sort ov a Roman, or a Feeld Marshal, ov himself with the ruuler, az he aulwaiz did befor delivering an adres. But thair feerz wer nuthing tu thair astonishment when he caim out with the story that Oeld Cheeseman "so long our respected frend and felo pilgrim in the plezant plainz ov nolej," az he cauld him—O yes! I dair sai! much ov that!—woz the orfan chield ov a disinherited yung laidy hu had marid against her faather'z wish, and huuz yung huzband had died, and hu had died ov soro herself, and huuz unfortyunait baiby (Oeld Cheeseman) had been braut up at the cost ov a grandfaather hu wood never consent

tu se it, baiby, boi or man : which grandfaather
woz nou ded, and surv him riet—that's *mi*
pooting in—and which grandfaather'z larj pro-
perty, thair being no wil, woz nou, and aul
ov a suden, and for ever, Oeld Cheeseman'z!
Our so long respected frend and felo pilgrim
in the plezant plainz ov nolej, the Reverend
wound up a lot ov bothering cwoetaishonz bi
saiing, wood "cum amung us wuns mor" that
dai fortniet, when he dezierd tu taic leev ov
us himself, in a more particyular maner.   With
theez wurdz, he staird seveerly round at our
feloez, and went solemly out.

Thair woz preshus consternaishon amung
the memberz ov the Soesiety, nou. Lots ov them
wonted tu rezien, and lots mor began tu tri
tu maic out that thai had never belongd tu it.
Houever, the Prezident stuc up, and sed that
thai must stand or faul tugether, and that if
a breech woz maid it shood be oever hiz
body—which woz ment to eucuraj the Soesiety :
but it didn't. The Prezident further sed, he
wood consider the pozishon in which thai
stood, and wood giv them hiz best opinion

and advies in a fyu daiz. This woz eegerly looct for, az he nyu a good deel ov the wurld on acount ov hiz faather'z being in the West Indies.

Aafter daiz and daiz ov hard thincing, and drauing armiz aul oever hiz slait, the Prezident cauld our feloez tugether, and maid the mater cleer. He sed it woz plain that when Oeld Cheeseman caim on the apointed dai, hiz furst revenj wood be tu impeech the Soesiety, and hav it flogd aul round. Aafter witnesing with joi the tortyur ov hiz enemiz, and gloeting oever the criez which agony wood ecstort from them, the probability woz that he wood inviet the Reverend, on pretens ov conversaishon, intu a prievit room—sai the parlor intu which pairents wer shoen, whair the tu grait gloebz wer which wer never yuezd—and wood thair reproech him with the vairius fraudz and opreshonz he had endyuerd at hiz handz. At the cloez ov hiz obzervaishonz he wood maic a signal tu a Priezfieter conseeld in the pasaj, hu wood then apeer and pich intu the Reverend, til he woz left insensibl. Oeld Cheeseman wood then maic Jane a prezent ov from fiev tu ten poundz, and wood leev the establishment in feendish triumf.

The Prezident ecsplaind that against the parlor part, or the Jane part, ov theez arainjments he had nuthing tu sai, but, on the part ov the Soesiety, he counseld dedly resistans. With this vyu he recomended that aul availabl descs shood be fild with stoenz, and that the furst wurd ov the complaint shood be the signal tu every felo tu let fli at Oeld Cheeseman. The boeld advies poot the Soesiety in beter spirits, and woz yunanimusly taicen. A poest about Oeld Cheeseman'z siez woz poot up in the plaiground, and aul our feloez practist at it til it was dinted aul oever.

When the dai caim, and plaisez wer cauld, every felo sat doun in a trembl. Thair had been much discusing and dispyueting az tu hou Oeld Cheeseman wood cum; but it woz the jeneral opinion that he wood apeer in a sort ov triumfal car draun bi for horsez, with the livery survants in front, and the Priezfieter in disgiez up behiend. So aul our feloez sat lisening for the sound ov wheelz. But no wheelz wer hurd, for Oeld Cheeseman wauct aafter aul, and caim intu the scuul without eny preparaishon. Prety much az he yuest tu be, oenly drest in blac.

"Jentlmen," sed the Reverend, prezenting him, "our so long respected frend and felo pilgrim in the plezant plainz ov nolej, iz dezierus tu ofer a wurd or tu. Atenshon, jentlmen, wun and aul!"

Every felo stoel hiz hand intu hiz desc and looct at the Prezident. The Prezident woz aul redy, and taicing aim at Oeld Cheeseman with hiz iez.

Whot did Oeld Cheeseman then, but wauc up tu hiz oeld desc, looc round him with a cweer smiel az if thair woz a teer in hiz i, and begin in a cwaivering mield vois, "Mi deer companionz and oeld frendz!"

Every felo'z hand caim out ov hiz desc, and the Prezident sudenly began tu cri.

"Mi deer companionz and oeld frendz," sed Oeld Cheeseman, "yu hav hurd ov mi good fortyun. I hav paast so meny yeerz under this ruuf—mi entier lief so far, I mai sai—that I hoep yu hav been glad tu heer ov it for mi saic. I cood never enjoi it without ecschainjing congratyulaishonz with yu. If we hav ever misunderstood wun anuther at aul, prai mi deer boiz let us forgiv and forget. I hav a grait tendernes for yu and I am shuur yu return it. I wont in the fulnes ov a graitful hart tu shaic handz with yu every wun. I hav cum bac tu du it, if yu pleez, mi deer boiz."

Sins the Prezident had begun tu cri, several uther felocz had broecen out heer and thair; but nou, when Oeld Cheeseman began with him az furst boi, laid hiz left hand afecshonatly on hiz shoelder and gaiv him hiz riet; and when the Prezident sed, "Indeed I doen't dezurv it; upon mi onor I doen't," thair woz sobing and criing aul oever the scuul. Every uther felo sed he didn't dezurv it, much in the saim wai; but Oeld Cheeseman, not miending that a bit, went cheerfuly round tu every boi, and wound up with every maaster—finishing of the Reverend laast.

Then a sniveling litl chap in a corner, hu

woz aulwaiz under sum punishment or uther, set up a shril cri ov "Sucses tu Oeld Cheeseman! Hoorai!" The Reverend glaird upon him, and sed, "*Mr* Cheeseman, sur." But, Oeld Cheeseman protesting that he liect hiz oeld naim a grait deel beter than hiz nyu wun, aul our feloez tooc up the cri; and, for I doen't no hou meny minits, thair woz such a roring ov Oeld Cheeseman, az woz never hurd.

Aafter that, thair woz a spred in the dieningroom ov the moest magnifisent ciend. Foulz, tungz, prezurvz, fruuts, confecshoneriz, jeliz, neegusez, barly shoogar templz, trieflz, cracerz —eet aul yu can and pocet aul yu liec— aul at Oeld Cheeseman'z ecspens. Aafter that, speechez, hoel holidai, dubl and trebl sets ov aul manerz ov thingz for aul manerz ov gaimz, donciz, poeny shaizez and driev yuerself, diner for aul the maasterz at the Seven Belz (twenty poundz a hed our feloez estimaited it at), an anyual holidai and feest ficst for that dai every yeer, and anuther on Oeld Cheeseman'z burthdai—Reverend bound doun befor aul the

feloez tu alou it, so that he cood never bac out
—aul at Oeld Cheeseman'z ecspens.

And didn't our feloez go doun in a body and
cheer outsied the Seven Belz? O no!

But thair'z sumthing els besiedz. Doen't
looc at the necst story teler, for thair'z mor
yet. Necst dai, it woz rezolvd that the Soesiety
shood maic it up with Jane, and then be
dizolvd. Whot du yu thinc ov Jane being gon,
tho! " Whot, gon for ever?" sed our feloez,
with long faisez. " Yes, tu be shuur," woz aul
the aanser thai cood get. Nun ov the peepl about
the hous wood sai enithing mor. At length,
the furst boi tooc upon himself tu aasc the
Reverend whether our oeld frend Jane woz realy
gon? The Reverend (he haz got a dauter at
hoem—turn-up noez, and red) replied seveerly,
"Yes, sur, Miss Pitt iz gon." The iedea of
cauling Jane Miss Pitt! Sum sed she had been
sent awai in disgrais for taicing muny from
Oeld Cheeseman; utherz sed she had gon
intu Oeld Cheeseman'z survis at a riez ov ten
poundz a yeer. Aul that our feloez nyu woz,
she woz gon.

It woz tu or thre munths aafterwerdz, when, wun aafternuun, an oepen carij stopt at the cricet feeld, just outsied boundz, with a laidy and jentlman in it, hu looct at the gaim a long tiem and stood up tu se it plaid. Noebody thaut much about them, until the saim sniveling litl chap caim in, against aul ruulz, from the poest whair he woz scout, and sed, " It's Jane! " Boeth Elevenz forgot the gaim directly, and ran crouding round the carij. It *woz* Jane! In such a bonet! And if yu'l beleev me, Jane woz marid tu Oeld Cheeseman.

It sunn becaim cwiet a regyular thing when our feloez wer hard at it in the plaiground, tu se a carij at the lo part ov the waul whair it joinz the hi part, and a laidy and jentlman standing up in it, loocing oever. The jentlman woz aulwaiz Oeld Cheeseman, and the laidy woz aulwaiz Jane.

The furst tiem I ever sau them, I sau them in that wai. Thair had been a good meny chainjez amung our feloez then, and it had turnd out that Bob Tarter'z faather wozn't wurth Milionz! He wozn't wurth enithing. Bob had gon for a soeljer, and Oeld Cheeseman had purchast his discharj. But that's not the carij. The carij stopt, and aul our feloez stopt as sunn az it woz seen.

"So yu hav never sent me tu Coventry aafter aul!" sed the laidy, laafing, az our feloez swormd up the waul tu shaic handz with her. "Ar yu never going tu du it?"

"Never! Never! Never!" on aul siedz.

I didn't understand whot she ment then, but ov cors I du nou. I woz very pleezd with her fais, tho, and with her good wai, and I coodn't help loocing at her—and at him tu—with aul our feloez clustering so joifuly about them.

Thai suun tooc noetis ov me az a nyu boi, so I thaut I miet az wel sworm up the waul mieself, and shaic handz with them az the rest did. I woz cwiet az glad tu se them az the rest wer, and woz cwiet az familiar with them in a moement.

"Oenly a fortniet nou," sed Oeld Cheeseman, "tu the holidaiz. Hu stops? Enibody?"

A good meny fingerz pointed at me, and a good meny voisez cried "He duz!" For it woz

F

2

Simplified Spelling

the yeer when yu wer aul awai; and raather lo
I woz about it, I can tel yu.

"O l" sed Oeld Cheeseman. "But it's solitary heer in the holidai tiem. He had beter cum
tu us."

So I went tu thair delietful hous, and woz az
hapy az I cood posibly be. Thai understand hou
tu conduct themselvz tuwordz boiz, *thai* du.
When thai taic a boi tu the plai, for instans,
thai *du* taic him. Thai doen't go in aafter it's
begun, or cum out befor it's oever. Thai no
hou tu bring a boi up, tu. Looc at thair oen.
Tho he iz very litl az yet, whot a capital boi he
iz! Whi, mi necst faivorit tu Mrs Cheeseman
and Oeld Cheeseman iz yung Cheeseman.

So, nou I hav toeld yu aul I no about Oeld
Cheeseman. And it's not much aafter aul, I am
afraid, iz it?

THE DIEVERTING HISTORY OV JOHN GILPIN

SHOING HOU HE WENT FARTHER THAN HE INTENDED, AND CAIM SAIF HOEM AGAIN

BI WILLIAM COWPER

JOHN GILPIN woz a sitizen
    Ov credit and renoun,
A trainband captin eec woz he
    Ov faimus London toun.

John Gilpin'z spouz sed tu her deer:
    " Tho weded we hav been
Theez twies ten teedius yeerz, yet we
    No holidai hav seen.

" Tumoro iz our weding dai,
    And we wil then repair
Untu the Bel at Edmonton,
    Aul in a shaiz and pair.

" Mi sister, and mi sister'z chield,
  Mieself and children thre
Wil fil the shaiz ; so yu must ried
  On horsbac aafter we."

He suun replied, " I du admier
  Ov woomanciend but wun,
And yu ar she, mi deerest deer,
  Thairfor it shal be dun.

" I am a linendraiper boeld,
  Az aul the wurld duth no,
And mi good frend, the calender,
  Wil lend hiz hors tu go."

Cwoth Mrs Gilpin, " That's wel sed ;
  And for that wien iz deer,
We wil be furnisht with our oen,
  Which iz boeth briet and cleer."

John Gilpin cist hiz luving wief ;
  Oerjoid woz he tu fiend
That, tho on plezher she woz bent,
  She had a fruugal miend.

The morning caim, the shaiz woz braut,
But yet woz not aloud
Tu driev up tu the dor, lest aul
Shood sai that she woz proud.

So thre dorz of the shaiz woz staid
Whair thai did aul get in ;
Sics preshus soelz, and aul agog
Tu dash thru thic and thin.

Smac went the whip, round went the wheelz,
Wer never foec so glad ;
The stoenz did ratl underneeth,
Az if Cheapside wer mad.

John Gilpin, at hiz horse'z sied
Seezd faast the floing main,
And up he got, in haist tu ried,
But suun caim doun again ;

For sadltre scairs reecht had he,
Hiz jurny tu begin,
When turning round hiz hed he sau
Thre customerz cum in.

So doun he caim; for los ov tiem,
    Altho it greevd him sor,
Yet los ov pens, ful wel he nyu,
    Wood trubl him much mor.

'T woz long befor the customerz
    Wer syueted tu thair miend,
When Betty screeming caim dounstairz,
    "The wien iz left behiend!"

"Good lac!" cwoth he; "yet bring it me,
    Mi lethern belt liecwiez,
In which I bair mi trusty sord,
    When I du ecsersiez."

Nou, Mistres Gilpin (cairful soel!)
    Had tu stoen botlz found,
Tu hoeld the licor that she luvd,
    And ceep it saif and sound.

Eech botl had a curling eer,
    Thru which the belt he dru,
And hung a botl on eech sied,
    Tu maic his balans tru.

Then oever aul, that he miet be
 Ecwipt from hed tu to,
Hiz long red cloec, wel brusht and neet
 He manfuly did thro.

Nou se him mounted wuns again
 Upon hiz nimbl steed,
Ful sloely paising oer the stoenz,
 With caushon and good heed.

But fiending suun a smuuther roed
 Beneeth hiz welshod feet,
The snorting beest began tu trot,
 Which gauld him in hiz seet.

So fair and softly, John he cried,
 But John he cried in vain;
That trot becalm a galop suun,
 In spiet ov curb and rain.

So stuuping doun, az needz he must
 Hu can not sit upriet,
He graaspt the main with boeth hiz handz,
 And eec with aul hiz miet.

Hiz hors, hu never in that sort
   Had handld been befor,
Whot thing upon hiz bac had got
   Did wunder mor and mor.

Awai went Gilpin, nec or naut;
   Awai went hat and wig;
He litl dremt, when he set out,
   Ov runing such a rig.

The wind did blo, the cloec did fli,
   Liec streemer long and gai,
Til, luup and buton fanling boeth,
   At laast it flu awai.

Then miet aul peepl wel dissurn
   The botlz he had slung;
A botl swinging at eech sied,
   Az hath been sed or sung.

The dogz did barc, the children screemd,
   Up flu the windoez aul;
And every soel cried out, "Wel dun!"
   Az loud az he cood baul.

Awai went Gilpin—hu but he ;
  Hiz faim suun spred around :
He cariz wait ! he riedz a rais,
  'T iz for a thouzand pound !

And stil az faast az he dru neer,
  'T woz wunderful tu vyu,
Hou in a tries the turnpiec men
  Thair gaits wied oepen thru.

And nou az he went bouing doun
  Hiz reecing hed ful lo,
The botlz twain behiend hiz bac
  Wer shaterd at a blo.

Doun ran the wien intu the roed,
  Moest pitius tu be seen,
Which maid hiz horse'z flancs tu smoec,
  Az thai had baisted been.

But stil he seemd tu cary wait
  With lethern gurdl braist ;
For aul miet se the botlnecs,
  Stil dangling at hiz waist.

Thus aul thru mery Islington
　　Thoez gambolz he did plai,
Until he caim untu the Wash
　　Ov Edmonton so gai ;

And thair he thru the wosh about
　　On boeth siedz ov the wai,
Just liec untu a trundling mop,
　　Or a wield guus at plai.

At Edmonton hiz luving wief
　　From the balcony espied
Her tender huzband, wundering much
　　Tu se hou he did ried.

"Stop, stop, John Gilpin ! heer'z the hous ! "
　　Thai aul aloud did cri ;
" The diner waits, and we ar tierd ";
　　Sed Gilpin "So am I ! "

But yet hiz hors woz not a whit
　　Incliend tu tary thair ;
For whi ? hiz oener had a hous
　　Ful ten mielz of, at Ware.

So, liec an aro swift he flu,
   Shot bi an archer strong;
So did he fli—which bringz me tu
   The midl ov mi song.

Awai went Gilpin, out ov breth,
   And sor against hiz wil,
Til at hiz frend the calender'z,
   Hiz hors at laast stood stil.

The calender, amaizd tu se
   Hiz naibor in such trim,
Laid doun hiz piep, flu tu the gait,
   And thus acosted him:

"Whot nyuez? whot nyuez? yuer tiedingz tel!
   Tel me yu must and shal—
Sai whi bairheded yu ar cum,
   Or whi yu cum at aul?"

Nou Gilpin had a plezant wit
   And luvd a tiemly joec;
And thus untu the calender
   In mery giez he spoec:

"I caim becauz yuer hors wood cum,
  And, if I wel forboed,
Mi hat and wig wil suun be heer;
  Thai ar upon the roed."

The calender, riet glad tu fiend
  Hiz frend in mery pin,
Returnd him not a singl wurd,
  But tu the hous went in.

When strait he caim with hat and wig;
  A wig that floed behiend;
A hat not much the wurs for wair,
  Eech cumly in its ciend.

He held them up, and in hiz turn
  Thus shoed hiz redy wit:
"Mi hed iz twies az big az yuerz,
  Thai thairfor needz must fit.

"But let me scraip the durt awai
  That hangz upon yuer fais;
And stop and eet, for wel yu mai
  Be in a hungry cais."

Sed John, "It iz mi weding dai,
  And aul the wurld wood stair
If wief shood dien at Edmonton,
  And I shood dien at Ware."

So turning tu hiz hors, he sed:
  " I am in haist tu dien;
'T woz for yuer plezher yu caim heer,
  Yu shal go bac for mien."

Aa, lucles speech, and buutles boest
  For which he paid ful deer;
For, whiel he spaic, a braiing as
  Did sing moest loud and cleer;

Whairat hiz hors did snort, az he
  Had hurd a lion ror,
And galopt of with aul hiz miet,
  Az he had dun befor.

Awai went Gilpin, and awai
  Went Gilpin'z hat and wig :
He lost them suuner than the furst;
  For whi ? thai wer tu big.

Nou Mistres Gilpin, when she sau
    Her huzband poesting doun
Intu the cuntry far awai,
    She poold out haaf a croun ;

And thus untu the yueth she sed,
    That droev them tu the Bel,
" This shal be yuerz, when yu bring bac
    Mi huzband saif and wel."

The yueth did ried, and sunn did meet
    John cuming bac amain ;
Hnum in a tries he tried tu stop
    Bi caching at hiz rain ;

But not performing whot he ment,
    And gladly wood hav dun,
The frieted steed he frieted mor,
    And maid him faaster run.

Awai went Gilpin, and awai
    Went poestboi at hiz heelz ;
The poestboi'z hors riet glad tu mis
    The lumbering ov the wheelz.

Sics jentlmen upon the roed,
   Thus seing Gilpin fli,
With poestboi scampering in the reer,
   Thai raizd the hyu and cri :

" Stop theef! stop theef !   A hiewaiman ! "
   Not wun ov them woz myuet ;
And aul and eech that paast that wai
   Did join in the persyuet.

And nou the turnpiec gaits again
   Flu oepen in short spais ;
The toelmen thincing az befor
   That Gilpin ran a rais.

And so he did, and wun it tu,
   For he got furst tu tonn ;
Nor stopt til whair he had got up
   He did again get doun.

Nou let us sing, long liv the Cing
   And Gilpin, long liv he !
And when he necst duth ried abraud,
   Mai I be thair tu se !

Simplified Spelling Society

Date...19

To the SECRETARY, SIMPLIFIED SPELLING SOCIETY,
44 Great Russell Street, London, W.C.

I wish to be enrolled as ${}^{a\ Full}_{an\ Associate}$ Member of the Simplified Spelling Society, at an Annual Subscription of ....*, and beg leave to enclose my first year's Subscription.

Or, I wish to be enrolled as a Life Member of the Simplified Spelling Society, and beg leave to enclose as my Subscription the sum of ....**

Name ....

Occupation...

Address...

....

* The minimum is Five Shillings for Full Members and One Shilling for Associate Members.

** The minimum is Three Pounds for Full Members and Twelve Shillings for Associate Members.

CPSIA information can be obtained
at www.ICGtesting.com
Printed in the USA
LVHW01s1254180318
570243LV00036B/2357/P